CW01455072

Sam

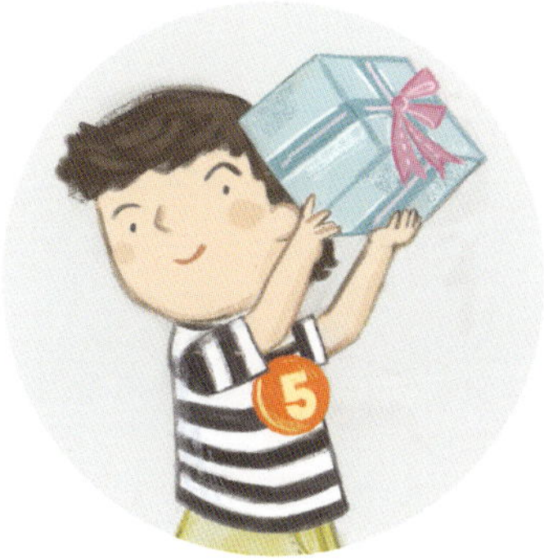

Kasia Reay

Illustrated by Lisa Molloy

Schofield&Sims

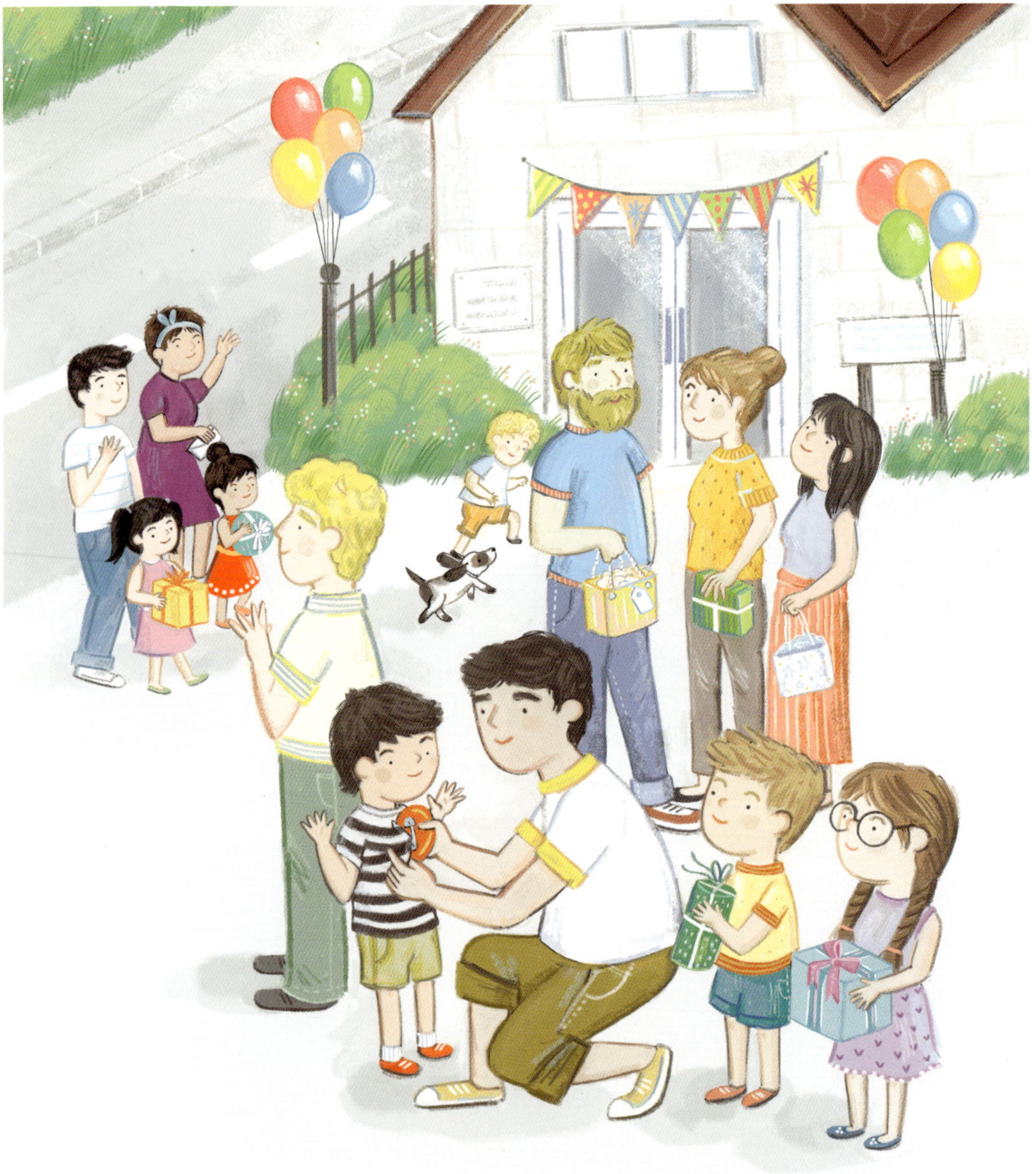

pin

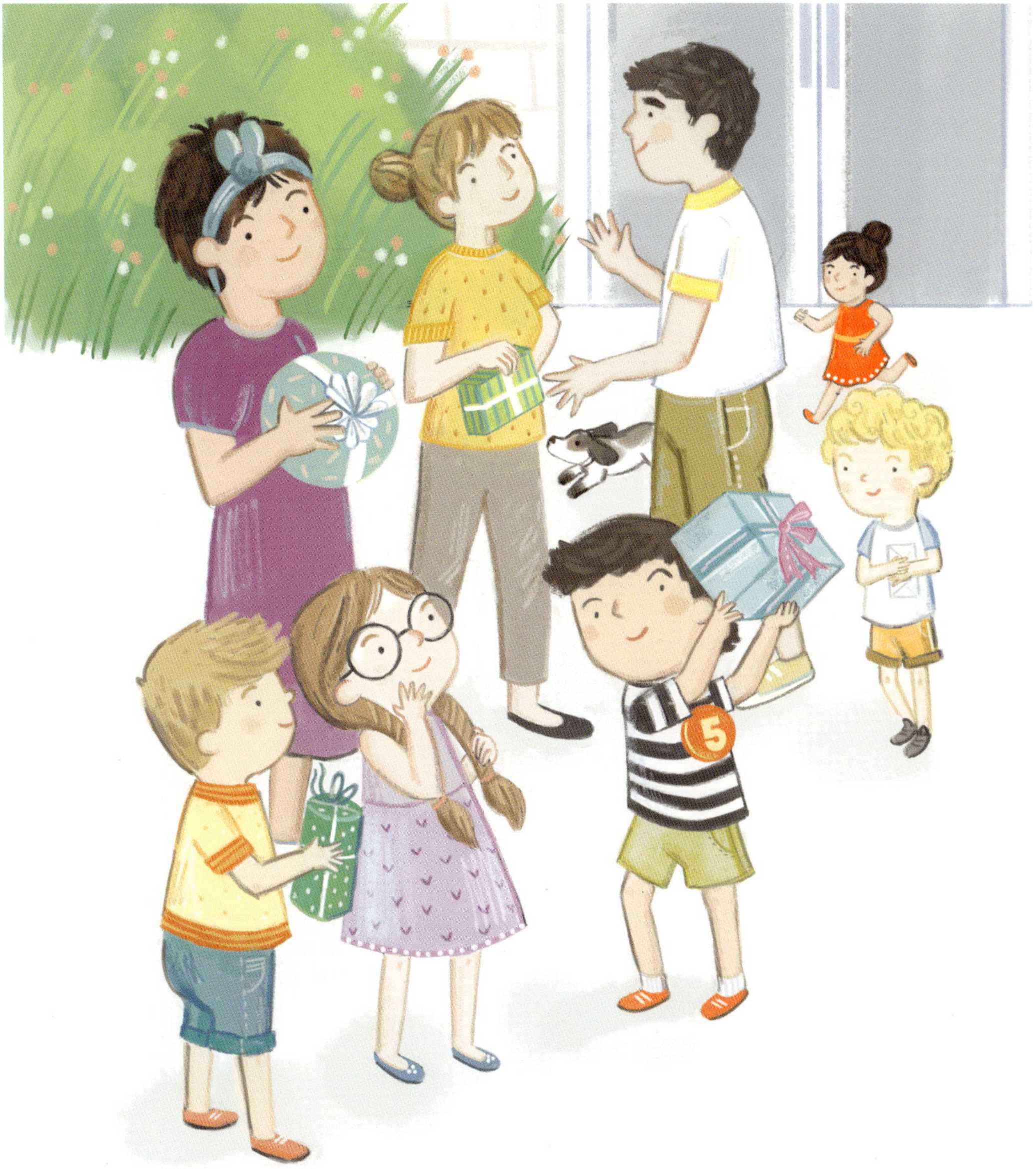

tip

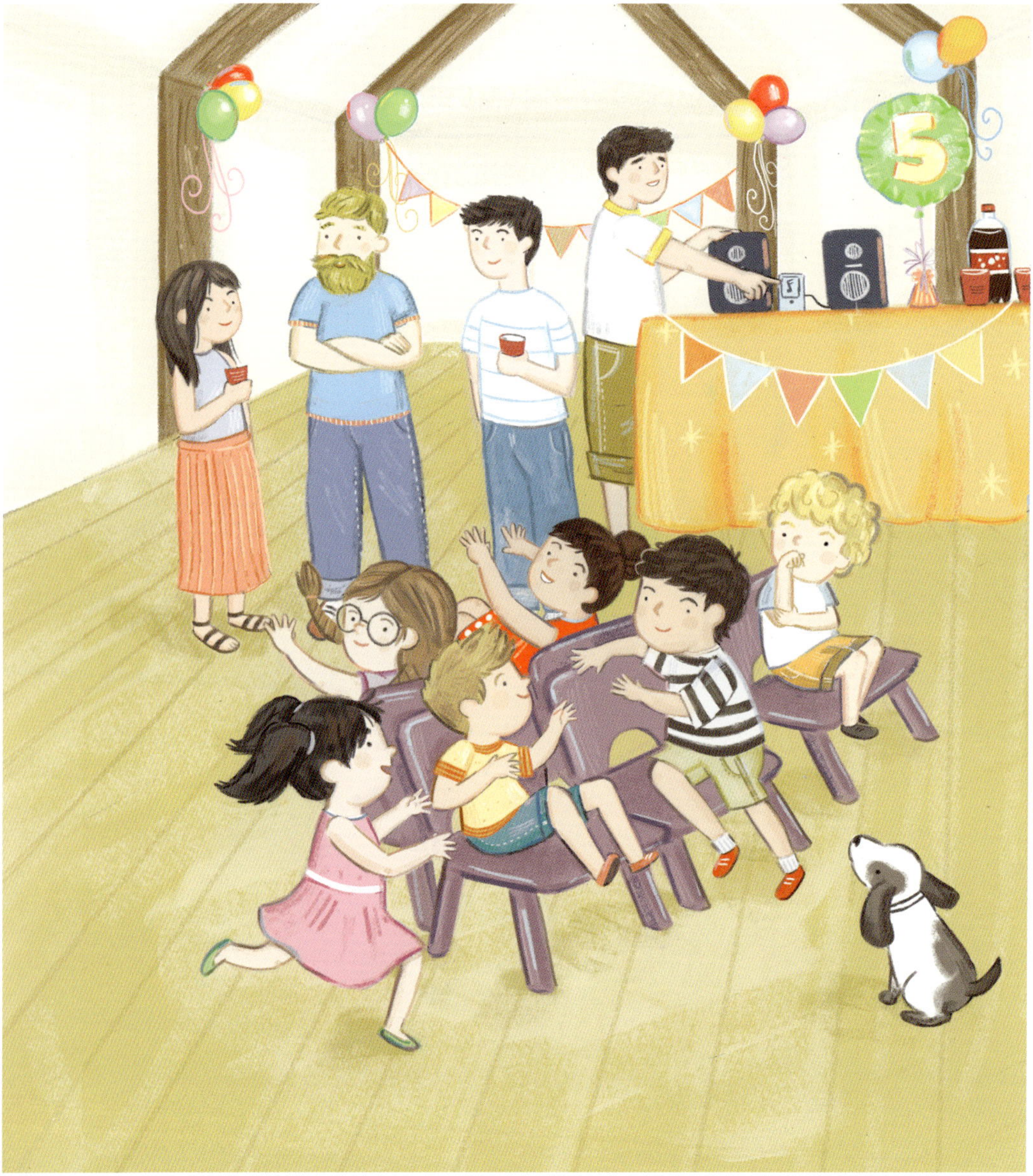

sit

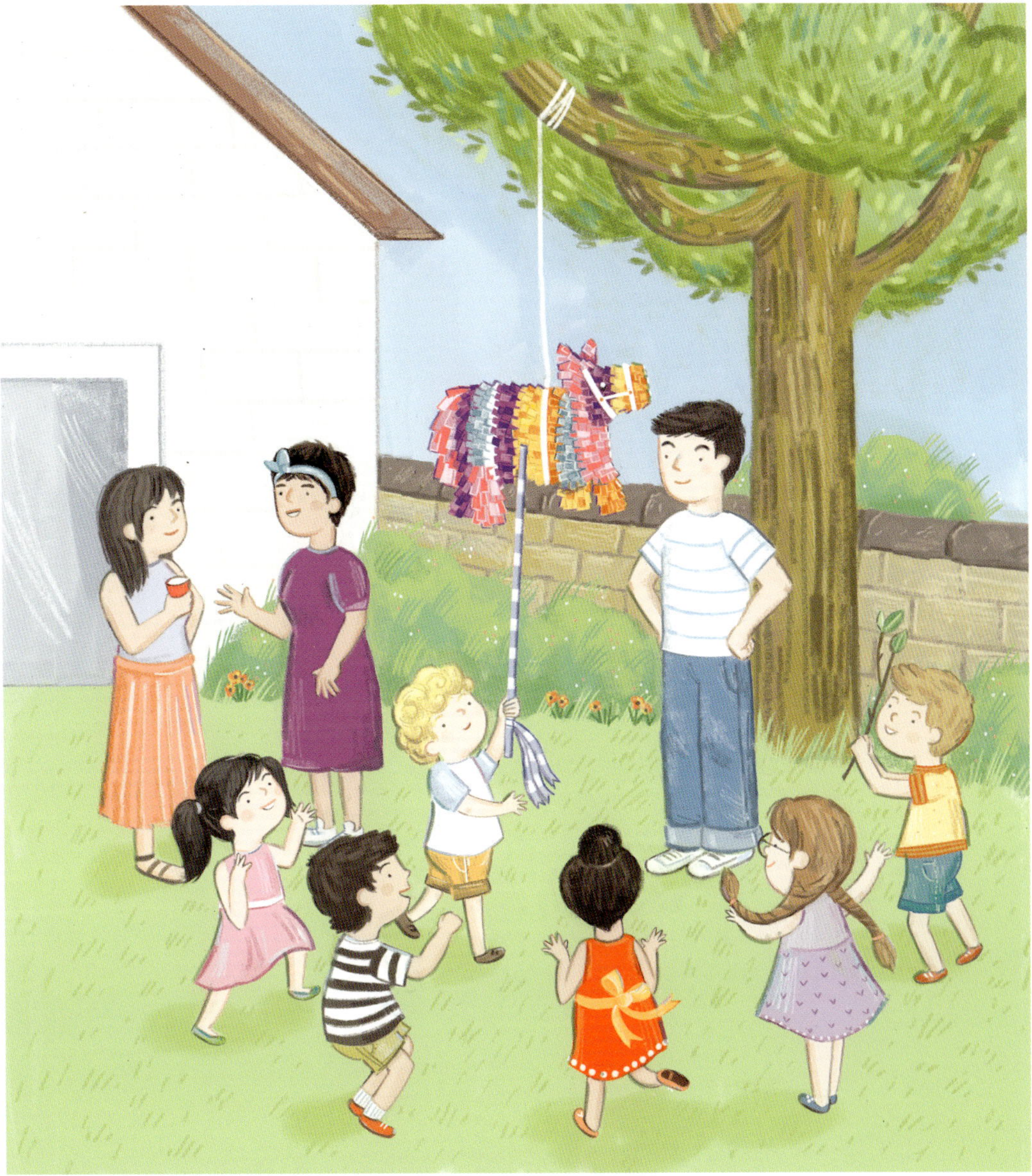

tap

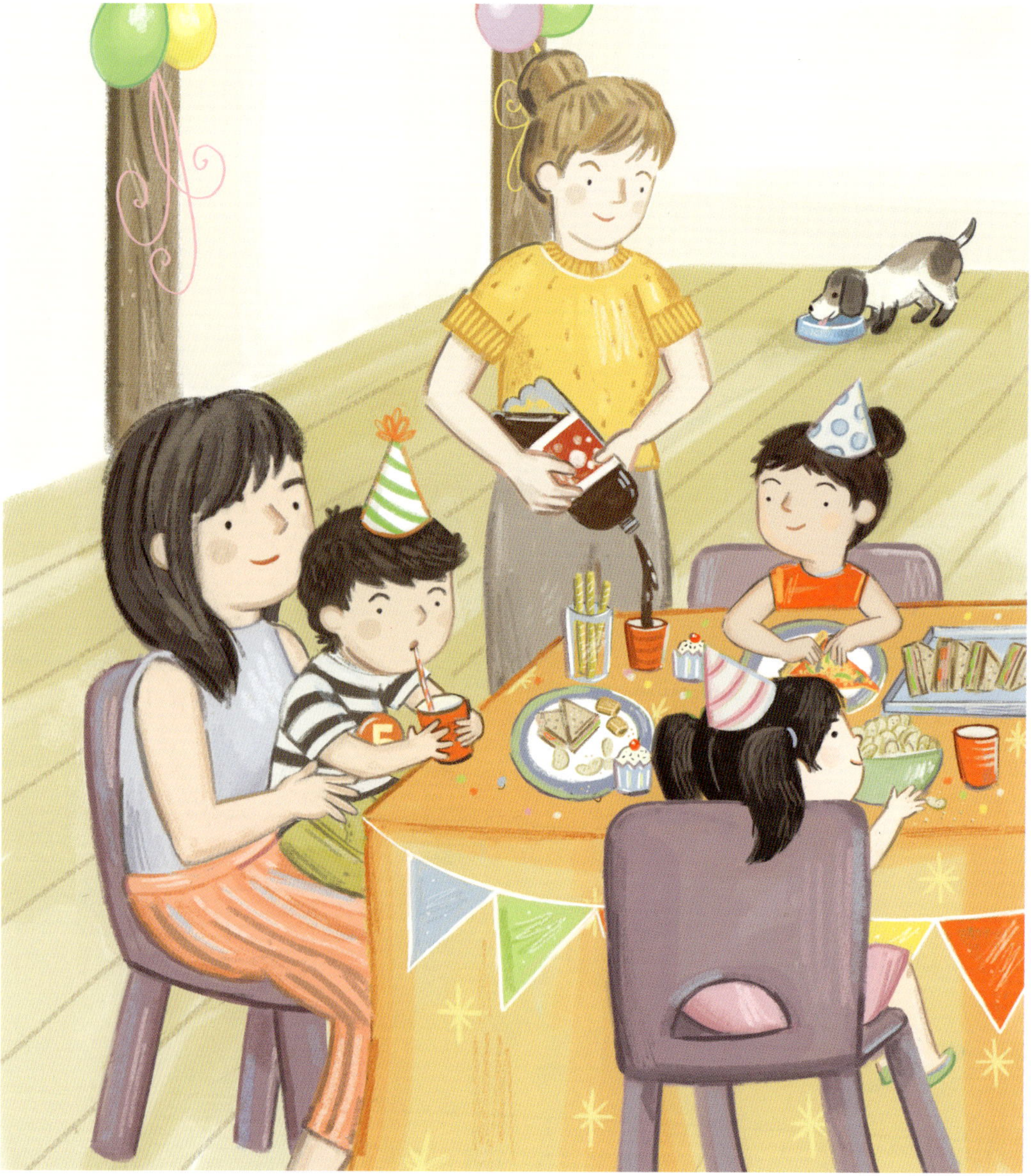

sip

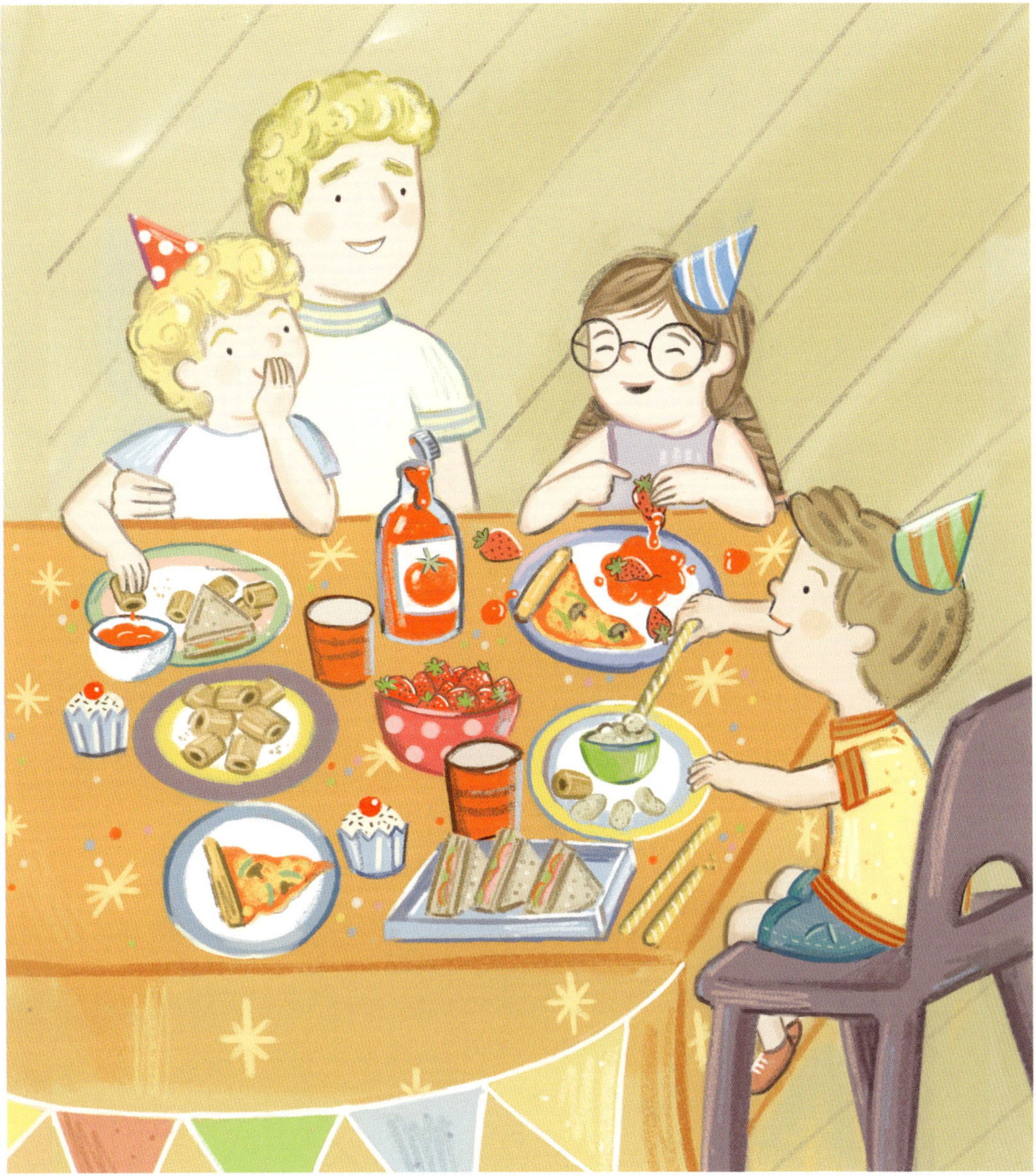

dip

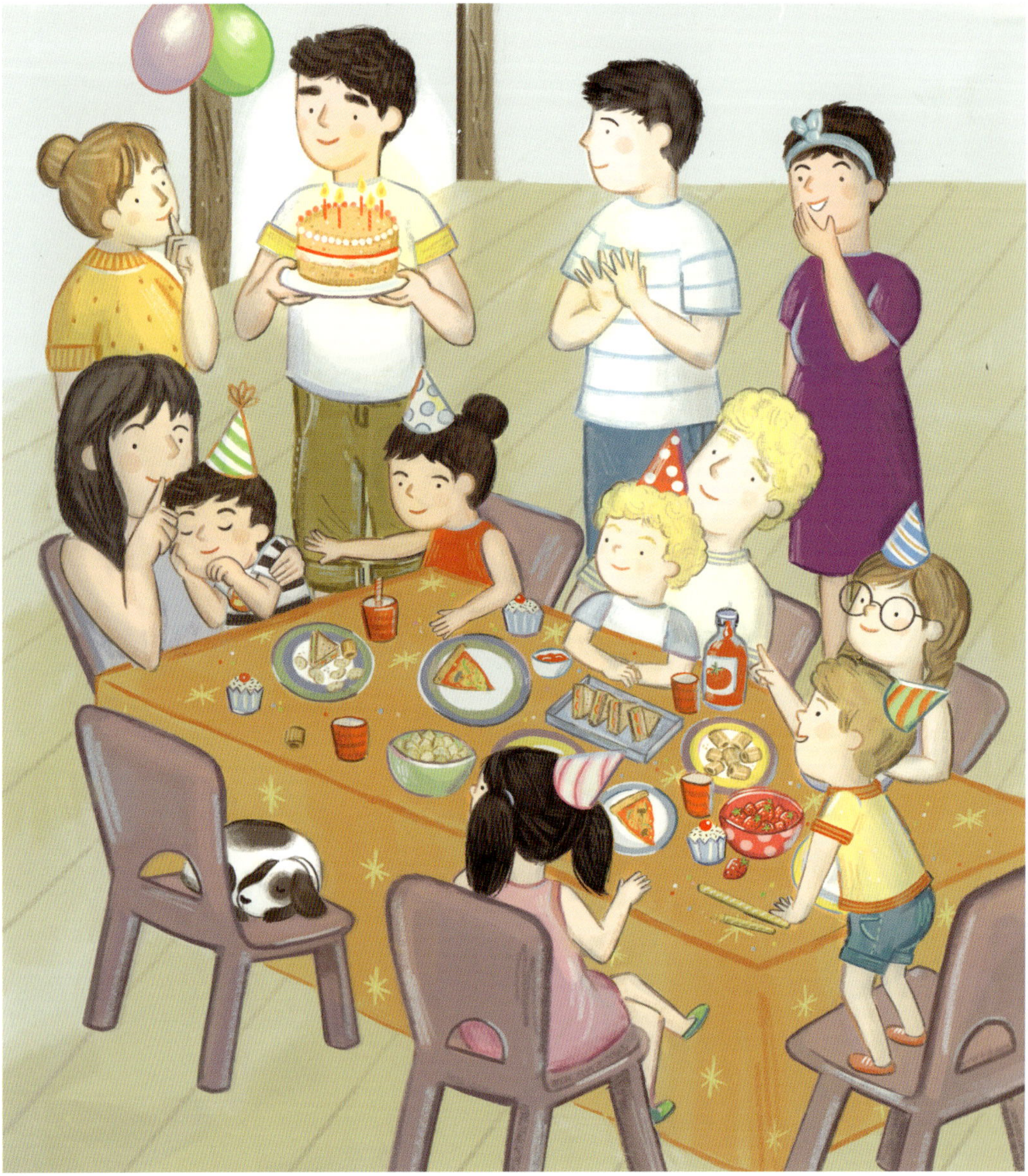

nap